SCORE READING
BOOK III — CONCERTOS

SCORE READING

BOOK III

CONCERTOS

BY

ROGER FISKE

MUSIC DEPARTMENT

OXFORD UNIVERSITY PRESS

WALTON STREET · OXFORD OX2 6DP
200 MADISON AVENUE · NEW YORK N.Y. 10016

INTRODUCTION

THESE books are intended for students of all ages who are interested in learning how to read an orchestral score. They are for use in conjunction with gramophone records. The two earlier books in the series (*Orchestration* and *Musical Form*) provided opportunities for score reading at a more elementary level. This third book is slightly more advanced, and covers the history of the concerto. It assumes that those who use it have also used its predecessors, or that they already possess some knowledge of instruments and of the way a score is set out. Some knowledge of form, in particular of sonata form, will be found helpful too, but this is not essential as some of the ground at least is revised in the pages that follow. As before, the choice of material has been limited by such factors as length and copyright. A modern work would have made the book more expensive, and would almost certainly have proved hard to follow. It can at least be claimed that this book covers two hundred years of concerto writing, and that it includes two complete concertos, besides eight single movements, some of which are of considerable length. All the music is frequently played in concert and radio programmes, and all of it is easy to enjoy. But it will be found that new and unexpected beauties are revealed to those who can follow the music with the eye as well as the ear. An index of the works provided, and a list of expression marks, will be found at the end of the book.

THE PRE-CLASSICAL CONCERTO

CONCERTOS are comparatively easy for score-readers as most of the interest is concentrated on a single stave, the soloist's stave; or, in the case of keyboard concertos, on a pair of staves. The pre-classical forms of the concerto were evolved in Italy towards the end of the seventeenth century and lasted until about 1750, the year Bach died. Throughout this period the soloists were almost always members of the orchestra; there was no such creature as the famous travelling virtuoso. For this reason passages of technical display were both uncommon and restrained, for no one wished to stagger an audience by personal brilliance. The main attraction of a concerto was simply the contrast between a soloist and a small group of players, or between a small group and a larger group. The *concerto grosso* commonly had three soloists, two violins and a cello (known as the *concertino*), and this small group was contrasted with the other players in the orchestra who might number a dozen or more and were known as the *ripieno*. Handel wrote twelve concertos of this type, his opus 6, but the first such set to achieve wide popularity had been Corelli's, published in 1714, the year after his death. Below you will find the first three movements of the eighth of Corelli's concertos, the one known as 'The Christmas Concerto'. Notice that in the first movement the soloists play the same music as the *ripieno* and therefore do not need staves of their own. In the second, the small and large groups are contrasted, though in fact their music is similar; the *ripieno* just stops playing every now and again. Only in the third movement do the soloists have individual parts which contrast with what is being played by the accompanying strings; even here the individuality is very short-lived. In addition, a harpsichord fills in the harmonies suggested by the figures under the bass line (see page 8).

Composers had a good deal of freedom as to the number of movements in a *concerto grosso*. This one has three more, two quick and vigorous, and a final one in gentle pastoral rhythm that to the original audience suggested the shepherds piping to their flocks at Christmas; hence the title of the work.

Concerto Grosso No. 8

I

Arcangelo Corelli
1653-1713

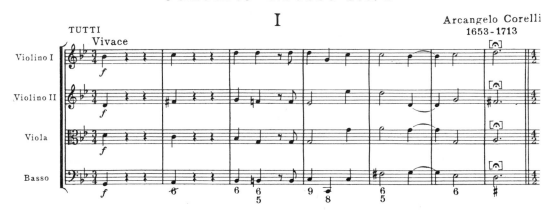

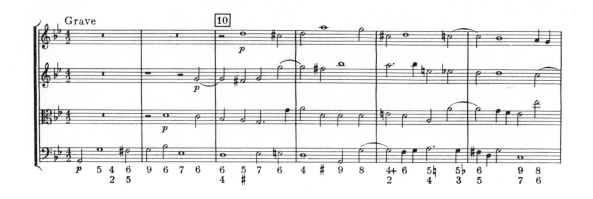

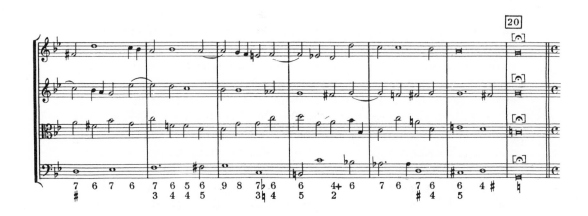

II

III

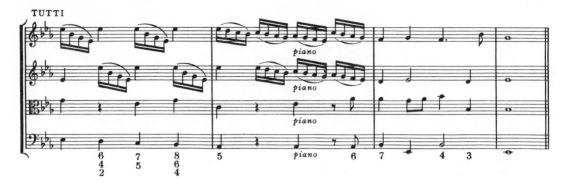

The solo concerto was developed alongside the *concerto grosso*. Bach seems to have been the only composer to write solo harpsichord concertos; his contemporaries presumably thought the instrument was too easily drowned by a string accompaniment. But Handel wrote a number of organ concertos, and solo violin concertos were especially popular. Bach's concertos were nearly always in three movements: fast, slow, fast. But Handel allowed himself more freedom.

The whole of Handel's oboe concerto in B flat is reproduced in the pages that follow. You will seldom need to look at more than the top two staves, the oboe solo and the first violins. Both the first and third movements begin with the first violins singing the main tune and the soloist then repeating it; this has always been a fundamental device in concerto-writing. Notice that the solo oboe is treated as a member of the orchestra. In the last movement he doubles the violins from beginning to end, and so has no real solo part at all. Notice also that the accompaniment must include a continuo instrument, either harpsichord or organ, to fill in the harmonies in such passages as lines 2 to 3 in the second movement. Such music would sound very thin if only the oboe and bass strings played, and this was not what Handel intended. The continuo player had the bass part in front of him and the figures underneath it showed him what chords to play above it; if there were no figures, he assumed a 'common' chord was needed. A Siciliana (third movement) is a slow dance in dotted six-eight rhythm.

The first movement of Bach's Violin Concerto in A minor (see page 15) also needs a harpsichord continuo for such passages as bars 29–31, though no figures seem to have survived. Bach's usual practice is to have a long tune at the start (often with all the instruments in unison), and again at the very end; in between come fragments of it in various keys, interspersed with episodes in which the soloist plays something new. In this A minor Violin Concerto his big opening theme (bars 1 to 24) ends in the dominant, so he cannot have it exactly the same at the end or his movement would finish in the wrong key. Accordingly he breaks it up, which makes it longer (bars 143–71), and this allows him to change key in the middle and get back to A minor. Between these main statements of the main tune, the accompanying strings try out the first few bars of it in C major (bar 52), D minor (bar 102), and A minor (bar 123; a false start!). But even in the intervening episodes the orchestra frequently uses the opening figure of the movement for its accompaniment; for instance in bar 25, and from bar 32 onwards. Notice too that the solo violin is still a member of the orchestra.

[8]

OBOE CONCERTO IN B FLAT BY HANDEL

Allegro.

|10|

[20]

SICILIANA.
Largo.

Vivace.

VIOLIN CONCERTO IN A MINOR BY BACH
FIRST MOVEMENT

THE CLASSICAL CONCERTO

THE principles of the classical concerto were evolved by a number of composers of whom John Christian Bach was among the first, and Mozart by far the greatest. We have seen that in the concertos of John Christian's father, Johann Sebastian Bach, the music usually stemmed from a single theme heard at the start. In the classical concerto it stemmed from *several* themes; thus there is more contrast. From about 1750 at least until 1830 the following scheme prevailed for first movements:

A The main themes played by the orchestra alone, and all in the basic key.

B The main themes repeated with the soloist joining in and taking the lead, and with a change of key (usually into the dominant) half-way through.

C The themes developed in various new keys.

D The recapitulation of the main themes as in B, but all in the basic key.

This scheme resembles that used in the first movement of symphonies except that the exposition (A) is repeated not note for note, but with two vital differences: the addition of the soloist, and the change of key in the middle. Mozart often makes other differences between A and B. Sometimes a tune that comes in the middle of A will be left out of B so that the soloist does not get at it until the very end of the movement. Often he will keep back one of his most attractive tunes for the soloist, omitting it in A and introducing it in B.

Often A ends with a climax which is broken off to introduce a short fragment of tune that is to remain the property of the orchestra. Towards the end of D, just before the orchestra reaches this fragment of tune, there occurs what is called the cadenza. This was an extemporization by the soloist on the themes of the movement, and ended conventionally with a trill which served to show the orchestra when to come in again.

The slow movement and finale of a classical concerto were planned on lines that were both simpler and less restricted.

The third of Mozart's four horn concertos is reproduced in the following pages. He wrote it in 1783. As in most scores of concertos, the solo part is put immediately above the first violins, a great convenience for the score-reader who at first will not wish to look at any other staves. The solo horn part is easy to find for it is the only one with no sharps or flats in the key signature. Its notes sound a sixth lower than printed. It happens that horns in E flat can be easily read by imagining the notes to be in the bass clef with a three-flat signature; but you will have to imagine them an octave higher than this suggests. The finale is a rondo. Only the first movement presents any problems; it is planned as follows:

A Bars 1–28; the main themes played by the orchestra. Notice the contrasting theme in bar 10 (still in E flat), and the little fragmentary theme in bar 25 (cf. bar 178).

B Bars 29–82; the main themes repeated by soloist and orchestra. In A they have only been hinted at; here they flower, the first of them into the memorable bars 33–36. The contrasting theme is now in the dominant (bar 52).

C The Development (bars 82–111) gets into the remote key of D flat via the little fragmentary theme. At this stage in his career Mozart seldom developed his themes systematically, but note the rhythmic figure in the first violins (bars 97–103) which we probably never noticed when it first came in bars 14–17.

D Bars 111 to end; the Recapitulation, with both main tunes back in the basic key. The cadenza comes at bar 171, and is indicated by the pause mark; Mozart provides the note on which the horn player must trill at the end of it.

Note: Clarinets (in B flat) sound a tone lower than printed; Fagotti are bassoons.

HORN CONCERTO NO. 3 IN E FLAT BY MOZART
K. 447

[130]

[140]

Romanze.

Allegro.

[180]

[190]

[200]

So far we have needed to look at little more than the solo line and the first violins. But Mozart in his later piano concertos made things more difficult for score-readers, and also much more interesting. He began to give the woodwind increasingly important parts, especially in his slow movements. Below you will find the slow movement of his most popular piano concerto, the one in A major which he wrote soon after *Figaro*. It is in the unusual key of F sharp minor. The contrasting tune in the middle (bar 35) comes first on the woodwind, and is in the relative major (A major). Mozart used to play his piano concertos himself, and often he did not bother to put down all the notes of the piano part, for he had them in his head. For instance, bar 66 cannot be complete; he must have played a quick arpeggio from the low G up to the high D, and most pianists do this today. Almost certainly bars 85–92 contain only a skeleton of what Mozart actually played, though not all pianists agree that there is any need to fill in here.

PIANO CONCERTO IN A MAJOR BY MOZART
(K. 488)
SLOW MOVEMENT

In the main, Beethoven followed Mozart in the way he constructed his concertos, though he tended to write at greater length. The first movement of his Piano Concerto No. 3 in C minor (written in 1800) is printed in the pages that follow.

A Bars 1–111; the main themes played by the orchestra. The first one begins softly on strings; notice the arch in the first two bars and the tonic-dominant rhythm in bar 3. Notice also the theme on the violins starting at bar 36. The main contrasting theme or 'second subject' begins in the wrong key at bar 50, and Beethoven seems to sense his 'mistake' for almost at once he pulls it back into his basic key of C (bar 62, flute and oboe). For his climax he reverts to his opening theme (bar 74; also 104 where it overlaps itself).

B Bars 112–249; the main themes rewritten for piano and orchestra. This time the main contrasting theme starts in E flat (bar 164) and stays there. Notice that from bar 199 onwards the orchestra is using the tonic-dominant rhythm of bar 3 for its accompaniment.

C Bars 249–308; the development, based on the first theme, in particular the bar 3 rhythm. Notice the first theme overlapping in canon (bars 267–9).

D Bars 309 to end; the recapitulation, with all the themes in the basic key of C (minor or major). The cadenza comes at bar 416. Pianists often play the one Beethoven himself wrote down, though it is not given in most scores. At the end of it Beethoven cocks a snook at the orchestra (and audience?) by having trills which in fact do not lead into the final orchestral passage; originally the violinists must have picked up their bows to come in with their final bars, put them down again when they found the trills leading nowhere, and then were probably caught out when the moment to play did arrive. In the final orchestral passage notice that the drums have the bar 3 rhythm.

Note: The piano part is always the one *without* a thick line on the left. Trombe are trumpets.

PIANO CONCERTO NO. 3 IN C MINOR BY BEETHOVEN
(Op. 37)

FIRST MOVEMENT

[210]

Note: After bar 233 players on the old horns had to take out their E flat crooks and put in C crooks.

[300]

THE ROMANTIC CONCERTO

AFTER Beethoven's death, composers usually dispensed with the orchestral opening to the first movement of the concerto; this enabled them to bring the soloist in right at the start. Examples: Mendelssohn's violin concerto and Schumann's piano concerto. (Brahms, however, still clung to the classical type of movement.) There was also a tendency to run the three movements of a concerto into one, and this was done by Mendelssohn in this same violin concerto, of which the slow movement is printed below. In his two piano concertos Liszt unified the movements to a much greater extent, using the same thematic material for more than one section.

The great change in concerto playing at this time was caused by the rise of the world-famous virtuoso; in particular of Paganini on the violin and of Liszt on the piano. Now for the first time in the history of instrumental music people crowded to hear the performer rather than the music. Naturally the solo parts in concertos became much more difficult so that these great virtuosi could show themselves off to better advantage. It was at this same time (c. 1840 onwards) that composers and performers drifted apart. In classical times a concerto was nearly always played by the man who had composed it.

A solo violin is much more easily drowned by orchestral accompaniment than is a solo piano. Notice how very lightly Mendelssohn accompanies his violin in the music below; also how he exploits the high ethereal notes at the top of the compass. Notice also the 'double-stopping' (two notes at once) in bars 55–78.

Grieg wrote his only concerto in 1868 when he was twenty-five. At the very end of his life, in 1906, he rewrote some of the orchestral part, considerably improving it. For instance, the second subject of the first movement (bar 49) had been a trumpet solo; it was Liszt who suggested making it a cello solo instead. The score of the first movement reproduced on page 88 includes almost all the alterations, though it has only two horns; the final version of the work had four.

Being a romantic concerto, there is no orchestral section at the start.

Bars 1–86; the Themes. The *first* comes at bar 7 and contains two contrasting moods, the first rhythmic (follow the oboes) and the second (bar 11) lyrical. The *second* theme (bar 49), like the first, comes on the orchestra (cellos) and is then repeated by the piano. There is a *third* theme (bar 73) for orchestra, which serves to end this part of the movement on a climax. Compare its opening with the piano entry in bar 2.

Bars 87–116; the Development. Flute and then horn try out the rhythmic part of the first theme, and oboe and cello the lyrical. Note third theme on piano in bar 110.

Bars 117 to end; the Recapitulation. All three themes in the basic key of A (minor or major). The cadenza (bar 176) is written out by the composer, as in many romantic concertos (for instance Mendelssohn's for violin); this prevents soloists who are poor composers from spoiling the music with something third-rate of their own. Grieg's cadenza is based on the first theme, the rhythmic part from bar 177 onwards, the lyrical part from bar 191.

VIOLIN CONCERTO IN E MINOR BY MENDELSSOHN
SLOW MOVEMENT

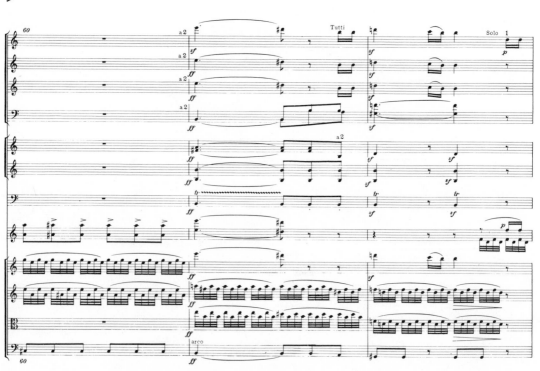

PIANO CONCERTO IN A MINOR BY GRIEG
FIRST MOVEMENT

B

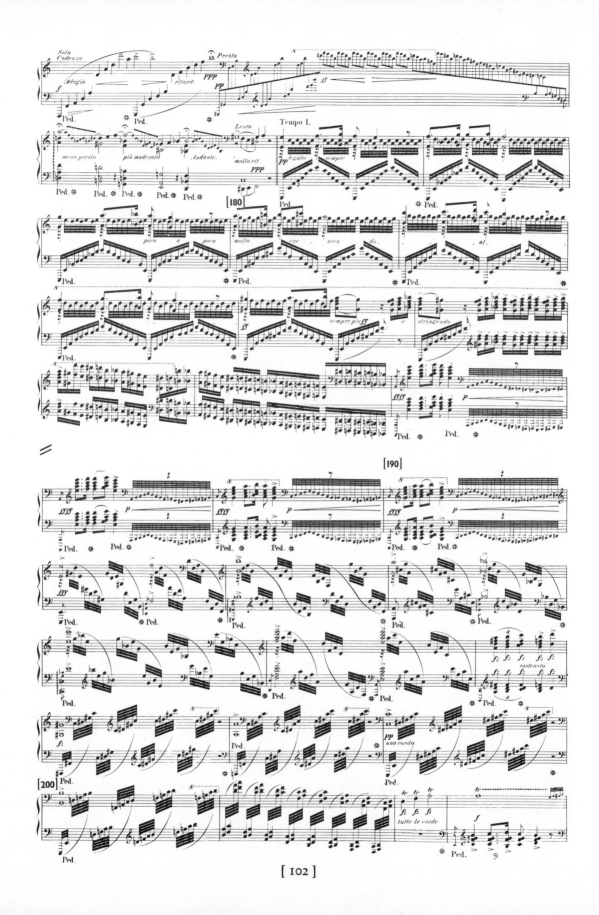

INDEX OF MUSIC

There are many excellent recordings of this music, and more appear every month. Some readers will be interested in the Pye recording of the Handel oboe concerto (CCL 30149); in this the soloist plays runs and flourishes additional to the notes set down by the composer, and this can be justified by the fact that all soloists in the eighteenth century improvised such runs and flourishes when playing concertos. But beginners in score reading may find this version confusing.

ACKNOWLEDGEMENTS

*Grateful acknowledgement is due to Penguin Books Ltd.
for permission to reproduce the slow movement
from their edition of Mendelssohn's Violin Concerto.
The first movement of Grieg's Piano Concerto is
published by permission of Hinrichsen Edition Ltd.,
London, the proprietors of Peters Edition copyrights
for continental Europe and South America*

EXPRESSION MARKS

Most composers use Italian words for their expression marks, and this is a great convenience, for musicians of all nationalities understand them

SPEED

Presto: very fast (*Prestissimo* is faster still)

Allegro: fast

Allegretto: fairly fast (much the same as *Andantino*)

Andante: at a moderate (or literally *walking*) pace

Lento: slow

Adagio: leisurely, i.e. very slow

Largo: slow and grand (*Larghetto*: not quite so slow as *Largo*)

These words can be qualified by *poco* (slightly, rather), *moderato* (moderately), *molto* (very) as in *poco allegro, allegro molto*; or by *più* (more), *meno* (less), *ma non troppo* (but not too much). *Sempre più allegro* means 'still faster'. They can also be qualified by the words in the section headed 'Style'. Note also *con moto* (with movement), *con brio* (with spirit).

Rit. (ritardando) ⎫
Rall. (rallentando) ⎭ getting slower

String. (stringendo) ⎫
Accel. (accelerando) ⎭ getting faster

These are cancelled by a new tempo indication, or by *a tempo* (in time, i.e. back to the original tempo)

STYLE

Agitato: agitated, restless

Animato: animated

Càntabile: with singing tone

Dolce (or *dol.*): sweetly

Doloroso: sadly

Espressivo (or *espress.*): expressively

Giocoso: cheerfully

Grazioso: gracefully (*Con grazia*: with grace)

Legato (literally *bound, tied*): the notes sound for their full length leading smoothly into each other without gaps; usually indicated by curved lines ('slurs') over or under the notes that are to be bound together; a form of punctuation

Leggiero: lightly

Maestoso: grand, stately

Marcato (or *marc.*): with emphasis, marked; *ben marcato*: well marked

Semplice: simply

Sostenuto: sustained tone

Staccato: the notes sound for less than their due length, with gaps separating them. Usually indicated by dots over or under the notes. The opposite of *legato*

Ten. (*tenuto*): 'held'; the player lingers on the note but only just perceptibly.

Tranquillo: calmly

Vivace or *Vivo*: lively

Pizzicato: plucked; *arco* (or *col arco*): with the bow

LOUDNESS

ff (*fortissimo*): very loud

f (*forte*): loud

mf (*mezzo-forte*): fairly loud

mp (*mezzo-piano*): fairly soft

sf (*sforzando*): accented
(sometimes *fz*)

con forza: with force

p (*piano*): soft

pp (*pianissimo*): very soft

cresc. (*crescendo*): getting louder

dim. (*diminuendo*): getting softer

morendo or *smorzando*: dying away

con (*senza*) *sordino*: with (without) mute

calando: getting both softer and slower;
calming down

CLEFS

All the above notes sound at the same pitch, 'middle C'. Violas use the alto clef, and sometimes trombones do too. Cellos and bassoons sometimes use the tenor clef if their parts lie very high; occasionally trombones use it.

TRANSPOSING INSTRUMENTS

CLARINETS if in B flat, the *sound* is *a tone lower* than you would expect.

if in A, the *sound* is *a tone and a half lower.*

(In classical music clarinets are sometimes in C, and this means that they behave normally. In German scores 'Clarinetti in B' means in B flat.)

HORNS   nowadays their parts are always written in F, and this means the *sound* is *a fifth lower* than you would expect.

(In classical music they were often in E flat—sounding a sixth lower—and other keys too. In German scores 'in Es' means in E flat.)

TRUMPETS nowadays either in C (when they present no problem) or in B flat or A (when they behave like clarinets). Occasionally in F.

Here are the first three notes of 'Three Blind Mice':

This is how a composer who wanted those sounds would write them for clarinets and for horn in F:

Keys with many sharps or flats are hard for the clarinet, so a composer would choose the clarinet in A. (N.B. Horn parts seldom have key signatures; each sharp or flat has to be specially indicated.)

Printed in Great Britain by
J. W. Arrowsmith Ltd., Bristol